FROM Boys TO Warriors

by Ronnie V. Nash

PAGE PUBLISHING, INC.
New York, NY

First originally published by Page Publishing, Inc. 2016

ISBN 978-1-68348-098-3 (pbk)
ISBN 978-1-68348-099-0 (digital)

Printed in the United States of America

Dedicated to those who have lost their lives in
combat their families and loved ones.
To the Missing in Action, we will not forget and to all those
serving and have served in our Military Forces.

Grant
I hope you enjoy the
book.
Best Wishes
Ronnie V. Nash

DEPARTMENT OF VETERANS AFFAIRS
READJUSTMENT COUNSELING SERVICE
FRESNO VET CENTER
3636 North 1ˢᵗ Street, Suite 112
Fresno, CA 93726-6818
Telephone: (559) 487-5660

May 6, 2003

Ronnie Nash
2384 Rio Gabrillo Way
Hanford, CA 93230

Dear Ronnie:

I just wanted to take a few minutes to say thank-you for the use of your poems and your support of the Vet Center program. I have had a great pleasure in sharing your poems with our veterans who have found a lot of inspiration in your work. With the use of your poems many of our clients have been able to express their thoughts, feelings and word that they have long since buried because of their exposure to combat. Also, I want to say thank-you on behalf of the wives and children who have been touched by your beautiful work.

The use of your inspiring words have made my job of getting veterans reconnected with their emotions a lot easier. I hope that one day all Americans, veterans and non-veterans get a chance to be touched by your very inspiring work.

Sincerely,

Joshua Ray Bentley, M.A.
Readjustment Counseling Therapist
Director/Team Leader

DEPARTMENT OF VETERANS AFFAIRS
READJUSTMENT COUNSELING SERVICE
SAN DIEGO VET CENTER
2900 Sixth Avenue
San Diego, CA 92103
Telephone: (619) 294-2040

September 11, 2000

American Literary Agents of Washington, Incorporated
1229 G Street, NW, Suite 317
Washington, DC 20005

Dear Sir,

Mr. Ron Nash has reached deep into his heart and soul to create poetry from the ravages of the Vietnam War. Combat veterans who hear the succinct message of these poems are moved to tears. Memories of their own experiences come bubbling up, "I wish I could say it as well as Ron does.." is a common reaction.

With Ron's permission, I've been using his poems in counseling sessions as a therapeutic tool to help combat veterans begin to experience emotions, other than anger, that have been buried for many years.

The seeds of Posttraumatic Stress Disorder are evident in the poetry. Verses are keys to unlocking memories and feelings. They give veterans a chance to begin the healing process.

Men who have survived the Vietnam War have a special story to tell. Ron tells the story with wit and courage through his poems.

Sincerely,

Paula Rose RN, C
Acting Team Leader

JUST A SOLDIER

We're numb from the lighting,
our emotions are nil.
They will shoot up our bodies,
when we take that next hill.
We walk very softly,
our eyes are alert.
Any minute that bullet,
may slam us to the dirt.
Who are we?
Are we reckless and bold?
No, only soldiers,
doing what we are told.

BEER RUN

On the road to Ben Het, from the City of Kon Tum.
A three-quarter ton truck, that night met its doom.
A land mine it did hit, after making a beer run.
We were called to the sight, with our ammo and guns.
A Warrant Officer was hurt, the driver dead on the spot.
We arrived at the wreck, expecting the area to be hot.
Security was set out, then we cleared the sight.
The Viet Cong did their job, killed an American that night.

YOUNG PEOPLE TO WARRIORS

Many young people
during Vietnam,
Were trained in everything,
from rifles to bombs.
During the early years
of that bloody war,
None could have known,
what lies in store.
Young and reckless were we,
most without care.
On ships we did board,
then sent over there.
Those that returned,
it's hard for us still.
Many warriors we knew,
were brutally killed.

MEMORIES

What do you expect of me?
Stars and stripes of old glory.
Like my father, in a war years ago.
You trained me to kill, a formidable foe.
I did not quit, nor did I surrender.
You sent me home, how well I remember.
Home to the world, to be ridiculed and shamed.
If I sound angry, then you are to blame.
Years have gone by and I still see the faces,
of young men dying in those faraway places.
It's not your money or your pity I seek.
Just rest for my brothers and a good night's sleep.

COMICAL SOUNDS

The sounds in the jungle late at night.
Do not always make you feel fright.
I remember one night, comical to me.
We had a new man, just arrived in country.
The perimeter check we made about dark.
Then a sound that he heard, gave him a start.
"F—— you," it said. It carried through the night.
Just a lizard, I chuckled, no reason for fright.

AN OBSTACLE

I consciously didn't do it,
I now know that it's true.
If my enemy you were,
I learned to dehumanize you.
When I spoke or I wrote,
I never referred to you as a man.
You were an obstacle to me,
who could interfere with our plan.
To destroy you was a necessity,
I was trained to reach my goal.
If I was to think of you as human,
it would have destroyed my very soul.
In my mind you were the enemy,
I could only think of you as a thing.
If I considered you but an obstacle,
In my mind, less turmoil would it bring.

BEFORE THE FIGHT

Two corps mobile strike force, I was then in.
The "A" camps would call us, before the fight began.
We'd gather intelligence, get support on line.
All of these things, we would need in time.
Our troops were supplied, we'd move until night.
Everyone's thoughts, we're on the upcoming fight.
First set up the perimeter, then security set out.
The enemy might probe, claymores and flares set about.
Radio contact, we would make once again.
From intelligence gathered, the enemy's dug in.
First light we saddled up, ate something with our men.
Who would walked out in a body bag, who would be in?

I WAS DRY

The Montagnard people, I cared for a lot.
The highlands they knew, from them I was taught.
At night we did rest, three Montagnards and I.
Each had their position, to each other close by.
It was during the monsoon, they hated the most.
They were sure one day, I would give up my ghost.
In a body bag I slept, when the rain did come down.
Superstitions they were, I was dry on the ground.

COMBAT HUMOR

When men are in combat, for many a month.
The things that humor them, may give you goose bumps.
Give me some time, I'll explain, you will see.
Some of the things, that were humorous to me.
While sitting in ambush, getting close to the night.
An enemy courier and four guards came into sight.
"Don't do a thing," was the team leader's word.
"The signal, I'll give, don't tire till it's heard."
We sit waiting, for what seemed a long time.
The team leader moved out, further down the line.
When the enemy arrived, on the trail, our leader jumped.
Then click went his weapon, no lead did it pump.
Everything worked out and I smile to this day.
A round he did not chamber, "Oh shit," did he say.
My third trip to Nam, down by Long Hai.
We were training Cambodians, under a clear blue sky.
From snipers, we received tire, there number was three.
Then behind a banana plant, one stood we could see.
My thought at the time, what amateurs are these?
Through the plant we did tire, he came out swiss cheese.
This is humor you ask, yes, I am sure there is more.
Ask any Vietnam veteran, what made him laugh in that war.

MY FAILURE

I still see your face, standing there.

Your smile, so broad and without a care.

Then a few days later, while in the field.

The war exploded, it was all too real.

A round had found its way to your head.

In the blink of an eye, you lay dead.

Of your loss, I did not mourn right then.

Rage built up, I directed it towards them.

For months after that, I could kill not enough.

I told myself, you must stay tough.

I still don't feel, I revenged your death.

But this failure old friend, I must live with.

IT'S NO GAME

Listen young people. there's no glory in war.
Its bodies you'll count, if you want to keep score.
I was young once, to this game I would go.
Airborne, ranger, and special forces I can show.
After all of those battles and all of those fights.
Many years later, I don't sleep well at nights.
For my country, I would serve until my last breath.
If you're needed then join, but don't glorify death.

FEEL FREE

Although you have condemned me,
you may feel I was wrong.
Your feelings you can express,
that's why we are strong.
Some countries would not allow,
expression in this way.
In America, you have the right,
what you feel you can say.
If our country you won't fight for,
leave that to guys like me.
So what if we don't come home,
at least you feel free.

JOYRIDE

We were drunk in Pleiku, another sergeant and I.

It was way past curfew, when we said our good-bye.

It was too far to walk, so a jeep we did steal.

Down the road we did fly, with white mice on our heel.

Their country we here helping, they were mad and didn't care.

At the jeep they did shoot, trying to part our hair.

We raced to our compound, we knew we'd gotten away.

For we were going to the field, that very next day.

FINAL DRINK

To my fallen brothers, so brave and so stout.
I cannot change the way that it worked out.
Of these thoughts in my head, I cannot be rid.
Why were you chosen, to walk with the dead?
I still remember your faces, but not your name.
Try as I might, it makes me feel ashamed.
Why can't I remember, these soldiers who fell?
Will we meet again, is there a heaven or hell?
Somehow you must know, each and every one.
Though you were killed, by shrapnel or a gun.
Your memory will go on, of you I do think.
If there is another place, we'll have a final drink.

MEDALS

In that war long ago, medals I did receive.

A hero I am not, in this you can believe.

Ask any veteran, what their medals are for?

They choose not to speak, of the horrors of war.

For the valor medals I received, you may think I am glad.

I would gladly turn them in, if dead soldiers' life they had.

So when you see a soldier's medals, in his eyes you will see dread.

For every valor medal, someone else is surely dead.

LETTERS FROM HOME

Many years ago I served, in that war in Vietnam.
We all looked forward, to getting letters from home.
We would often joke, about comments made.
We'd make up our own answers, with us they stayed.
Like how are you? I hope you're doing well.
I'm doing just great, it's my first time in hell.
"Aren't you happy for Dad?" A new car he has again.
Well send it on over, well take it for a spin.
I'm so tired of the cold, it snowed again today.
It's 110 in the shade, send that snow our way.
Mr. Jones passed away, he owned the local store.
We lost some people too, all under twenty-four.
Then the joking would stop, no more would be said.
We didn't want to think, of those dying or dead.

FIRST TASTE OF COMBAT

I remember, my first trip to Vietnam.
Infantry I was and a little headstrong.
We were ready for battle, we had trained so well.
My first taste of combat, shot that all to hell.
As the rounds flew over and around me so close.
They knew I was scared, I turned white as a ghost.
So when I hear stories, of a soldier's first fight.
When he tells me the tale, of there being no fright.
This man I stay away from, him I do dread.
If he's telling the truth, he's either crazy or dead.

ENEMY

I don't even know you, my enemy you are.

I come from a land, that is distant and far.

I have left all my loved ones, for an enemy to meet.

There is nothing personal, I cannot retreat.

Our job as enemies, no matter which side.

Is to go into battle, for our countries' pride.

In the jungles and paddies, we fight for the land.

Our countries don't care, we're expendable to them.

So on into battle, we shall meet someday.

Destroying each other, that's the game enemies play.

FOR HER WE FIGHT

In our throat there is a lump,
when we hear our anthem played.
Many veterans, across our nation
know of someone, whose life was paid.
The country that they died for
was our own, ask anyone.
The stars and stripes, still wave proudly,
they cover all her long lost sons.
No matter where a soldier goes,
it's for old glory that he fights.
Support our people in uniform,
they may not see, the morning light.

HAVING FUN

When I first entered the army, they issued me a gun.

Playing war games at times, I felt would be fun.

A lot of classes I did go to, marching, running, and RT.

For a kid not yet eighteen, how much better could that be?

After basic and AIT, six months in Germany I did spend.

I volunteered for Vietnam, the fun would now end.

I was only nineteen, with real rounds in my gun.

Is it any wonder? I forgot how to have fun.

FOUL

I've heard it before,
and it's talked about still.
The atrocities in Vietnam,
by Americans you feel.
I'll tell you my views,
then I'll put it to rest.
Charlie, our enemy,
you never saw at his best.
You never walked into a village,
that Charlie left.
Was too friendly to Americans.
maybe accepted our help.
He'd decapitate the village chief,
A family member disembowel.
We may not have played fair,
against Charlie who yelled foul.

FRIENDLY FIRE

In seventy, we were starting a mission after Tet.

Preparing to launch from an "A" camp, Ben Het.

Then came a call, "Inbound choppers, on the way."

"Hey, Sarge, can you help us?" I heard someone say.

I went to give a hand, as the choppers came in.

What? I drag off those choppers, charred bodies of men.

In the path of Napalm, sixty Montagnards, did fall.

Dropped by our own aircraft, bombs, you can't recall.

This was done by friendly fire, another sergeant said.

I thought friendly or not, they're still just as dead.

HANDS

I look down at my hands, now much older than back then.

I know how I got every scar, how the bones were broke in them.

It's sometimes hard now to believe, the

things these hands have done.

I remember the very first time, these awkward hands held my son.

I remember too the bloody days, when I had to fight to stay alive.

These hands held a weapon, many enemy did not survive.

These hands have been destructive, but they have seen gentler days.

Holding my wife or my children, comforting

a soldier as he passed away.

These hands have no conscience, they do as they are trained.

They do what is required, I store the turmoil in my brain.

IF SHE KNEW

I know that I love her, of this I am sure.

My wife, I do speak of, with her I am secure.

Often I have wondered, would she care as much.

Could she bear to kiss me, or give a loving touch?

These things I have wondered, could she still do?

If the things that I've done, in combat she knew.

While walking together, would she still hold my hand?

If she knew that from them, ran blood from other men.

A gentle kiss would I still get at night when we retire?

If she knew from these lips, on the enemy, I called fire.

Would she care what I think, if my thoughts she knew then?

Killed the enemy, I have and felt nothing for them.

Would she rub my shoulders, when I come home tense?

If she knew, I cared not, the war made no sense.

This happiness, I don't deserve, she has brought into my life.

Love and support I do get, from this lady, my wife.

IT'S CRAZY

I was having so much fun, a couple months before.
Then I was fighting, in the middle of a war.
When you're young and bullheaded, death is no threat.
Then the rounds start flying, you break out in a sweat
It's crazy, say I, this thing they call war.
Men trying to kill me, I've never seen before.
After months of fighting, seeing the death and pain.
Something has changed, you think you're going insane;
Not for the death, or the fighting you've seen.
Feelings you should have, are replaced with nothing.

INSIDE SOMETHING DIES

A lot of death and destruction in my life, I did see.

Often times I have wondered, why them and not me?

Who makes the choice, of who lives and who dies?

In combat you know, when you look in death's eyes.

Though you know, he won't make it, comfort him you will.

You never wanted to know him, he might die on the next hill.

Though most won't admit it, in combat it's true.

If you see many battles, something dies inside you.

You can't get it back, I'm sure most will agree.

When you see a man hit, you think, better him than me.

A SLOW HURRY

I remember the last time
I served over there.
From the fighting I was numb,
I just didn't care.
I fought to stay alive,
the enemy I would bury.
We made our objectives,
always in a slow hurry.
This makes no sense to you,
I'll put it another way.
Our minds did race,
But slow our movements did stay.

JUST WE

We were brown, yellow, red, black, and white.
You called for our service, then trained us to fight.
Most were just kids, when we went to that land.
The war you'd like to forget, the one called Vietnam.
The color of our skin, didn't matter to me.
We protected each other, there was no they just we.
When we that returned, saw things still unjust.
You still had the nerve, to ask veterans for trust.

LAST STAGE

The question was put to me,
is it death that you fear?
Many times I have cheated it,
to live another year.
The end of one's life,
will bring sadness to some.
The families, the friends
and other close ones.
But fear it, I don't,
though I will not rush in.
Some people believe,
something new, will begin.
To my family, when I go,
let it cause you no strife.
Death is the last stage,
in this theater, called life.

THAT GUY

Remember that guy
we served with in 'Nam?
The one that was so proud
of his family at home.
That guy you ran around with
when you came in.
That guy that was always clowning,
liked to drink gin.
Remember the night
you guys were caught in the ville?
MP's brought you back,
you were both drunk as hell.
Whatever happened
to old what's his name?
I didn't know, I'm sorry
that is a shame.

LUCKY ME

Damn, I am lucky,
so I've been told.
Three tours in Vietnam,
and my body's not cold.
Yes, I was there,
a lot of battles I've fought.
Yeah, I'm lucky, I saw men die
without much thought.
I've walked into ambushes,
without a scratch I escaped.
Saw men shot to hell,
with mangled bodies or bodies draped.
Then I was sent home,
my mind was on the run.
You tell me,
who's the lucky one?

HE WATCHES ME

Just a young soldier, when my brother passed away.
What I'm about to tell you, I believe to this day.
I have no way of knowing, if you believe as me.
Full Native American, my grandmother, was she.
Proud of my heritage, I have always been.
Though belief in Indian ways, I didn't begin.
Until the death of my brother, Gary is his name.
At my side to warn me, I believe he came.
Hallucinations you may say, it had to be.
I choose to believe, he watches over me.

MY GHOSTS

Deep in the shadows, and crevices of my brain.
The memory, of what is long past, still remains.
Things I chose to remember, were of little concern.
Bad thoughts I shut out, so my mind wouldn't burn.
Age becomes an enemy, ghosts return from the past
A lonely feeling envelopes me, oh, how it does last?
To rid myself of that feeling, many ways I have tried.
Some methods that I used, caused loved ones to cry.
They couldn't understand, never could they come close.
The troubles that I've caused, still I have these ghosts.

MERCY KILLING

A soldier I knew, many years ago
His feelings, like a lot of us. he refuses to show.
This man's turmoil, is set in his head
He thinks of the battles, his comrades left dead.
Try as he might, he just can't forget
Some enemy tactics, that bother him yet.
During an ambush, they would shoot one man
Not to kill, but to wound, then the horror began.
The enemy knew, to save him we'd try
Wounded on the field, you could hear his cries.
When an attempt was made, they would fire again
Many more would be hit, trying to save a friend.
When the wounded man's cries, would finally stop
You would hear the crack of a rifle, hear the bones pop.
He would beg for relief, of his torture and pain
Then from one of his own, a shot to the brain.
The trigger was pulled, by this soldier I know
Never a word was said, for the mercy he showed.
He has lived man years, hearing the moans and the groans
He must left with the fact; he killed one of his own.

WARRIORS LOST

There are pictures on the mantels,
all across this great land.
Of loved ones who were lost,
in a country called Vietnam.
The families remember fondly,
of these warrior's childhood days.
Never should we forget.
the ultimate price that they paid.
When you see our country's flag,
raise your head and be proud.
For the warriors that were lost,
are saluting smartly from the clouds.

ROUGH LANDING

A resupply mission, I volunteered for.
Supplies we were to kick from the chopper door.
We dropped the supplies, thirty rounds she did take.
Back for the "A" camp, the pilot did make.
"Hang on," said he, "it's hard we will land."
The thought of death, was close at hand.
In like a fixed wing, sparks flew from the skids.
We all walked away, to a stop that pilot slid.

MY LADY

I would take her with me everywhere.
When I was young and over there.
Though a war we were in.
On her, I did always depend.
Like lovers, we stayed in the night.
At time with me, she would light.
Left her I did, in the blazing sun.
My life she saved, this lady my gun.

NOT ALLOWED

We weren't allowed
to just be boys.
Weapons we learned,
those were our toys.
Thirty years later,
you wonder why.
These Vietnam vets,
breakdown and cry.
Most work hard,
they try to endure.
For their depression,
is there no cure?

NO MORE

I heard many men say, in the Vietnam War,
"If I make it back home, I'll return no more."
I too made that remark, during my first trip.
On reality I felt, I was losing my grip.
Two years later, I volunteered and returned.
Even though on my first trip, half my body was burned.
I knew people that had died and been laid to rest.
Now new skills I had learned, did I need the test?
After my second tour, a third time I would go.
Many went less, some went more that I know.
After my third tour I wasn't finished yet.
I volunteered for Thailand, we had dead pilots to get.
Unarmed we went in, to retrieve our dead.
The sights that we saw, still fill my head.
Why was it I wonder, that I felt the need.
To return to that war, watch my sanity bleed.

OUT OF STYLE

I don't remember exactly when.
While I was gone, it must have been.
Patriotism, went out of style.
The war we fought, all the while.
During the war, in Vietnam.
An unpopular war, here at home.
In other wars, a different story.
We came home, they burned old glory.
Those days of old, I can't forget.
On my uniform, my countrymen spit.
I stand proud, when our flag does pass.
It angers me, if you stay on your ass.
It seems our history, some have forgot.
I respected more, the enemy I fought.

POLITICAL GREED

Never has this country,
fought a war like Vietnam.
Years we battled there,
many soldiers did not come home.
Often we would wonder,
is anybody keeping track?
We'd move an enemy from an area,
turn around and give it back.
It made no sense for politicians,
to run the war from a desk.
While the soldiers were the pawns,
in a game of political chess.
Soldiers returned from that war,
Each one gave their all.
Political greed extended the fight,
politicians let Vietnam fall.

RESPECT OLD GLORY

What's wrong with the people, in this great land?
Do they not realize, our flag is still grand?
Have they not heard, of the wars that we've fought?
Heard of all the men dying, is it all for naught?
Show respect for our hag, or the children won't learn
Forget those days of old when our flag they did burn.
Stand with your children, when old glory goes by.
When she's raised at our schools raise your head high.
If you live in this country, here you will stay.
Show respect for old glory, long may she wave.

WE REMEMBER YOU

In the Veterans Hospital I was sitting, in San Diego.

The reason I was there, started many years ago.

I felt at one time, in the military I belonged.

That warrior I am not, when I was young and strong.

I sit and wonder why, after all these years.

For all the warriors lost, it's hard to shed tears.

I looked around in the hospital, at many other vets.

Lost limbs and body scars, that war they won't forget.

Scarred though we are, to life and loved ones, we hang on.

We live for those who were lost, their memory is not gone.

RESPECT YOU EARN

Two corps MIKE Force, I was serving with then.
On the previous mission, we lost a few men.
With our yards we did drink, to pay our respect.
We were all drinking hard, trying to forget.
An officer walked in, supply was his field.
Attention he wanted, no one would yield.
Then he stated in a voice, both loud and clear.
No man would you have lost, had an officer been there.
Though I did know better, my career on the line.
That officer I did hit, some that died were mine.
Punished I was, fined and sent to Ben Het.
In combat, respect is earned that officer did forget.

WOMEN VETERANS

When a veteran is thought of, is it usually a man?
Women also serve proudly, for this great land.
Compared to the men, the women numbers are few.
In combat, these ladies have lost their lives too.
As enlisted and officers, these women have served.
For doing their job well, recognition is deserved.
To all women veterans, I say," Thank You, Ma'am."
I served proudly with you, for our Uncle Sam.

SELF-MEDICATE

Set up the perimeter, that clearing you see,
is for all the choppers, secure the LZ.
Thirty days in the field and back to Pleiku,
you will hear no laughter, we lost quite a few.
Those of us still walking after the fight,
will be in the club drinking tonight.
The barstools are full and you will hear not a sound,
we self-medicate ourselves till we can't hear the rounds.
Four days of drinking, drunk we will get,
we heard our next mission is up near Ben Het.
That man in the corner, leave him alone,
his team leader was killed, his body is going home.
You can tell the seasoned veterans, not by the glare,
look close into his eyes, he has that thousand yard stare.

WHEN TO FIGHT

Dak Pek, Dak Seng, Ben Het. Dak To,
Plei Me and Plei Mrong, I remember well.
From Pleiku, the MIKE Force are called to assist,
for the men at those camps, it was sometimes hell.
Another mission we've got. Where? It matters not,
we're ready, though our heads are not clear.
The enemy wants to play, it's a hot humid day,
I wish to hell, I hadn't drank all that beer.
In choppers we go in, saddle up, and move again,
we move cautiously, for the signs are all around.
The enemy thinks he will choose, where we will fight,
at day's end we're on yet, another piece of ground.
The perimeter is set up, flares and claymores set out,
for best effect the machine guns are emplaced.
Now at last we can eat and try to get some sleep,
if we are attacked, we will not be disgraced.
Trip flares and claymores go off through the night,
the adrenaline flows, not a single round is fired.
Our enemy we know, our position we don't show,
the enemy has learned, we'll fight, when we desire.

SOLDIER ON LEAVE

Home on leave, after a year in Vietnam.
Waiting for a flight, to take me on home.
In Seattle, I was, in class "A" dress.
Bloused boots, Green Beret and uniform pressed.
A little boy about five, walked up to me.
I looked and I smiled. "Hi, soldier," said he.
"Were you in the war? Are you going home?"
His mother then grabbed him, a look of pure stone.
Was her actions from my uniform, or was it fright?
Did she think, from Vietnam, I would bring the fight?
Then from her husband, "I apologize, for my wife."
But that incident I'll remember, the rest of my life.

WHY BASIC TRAINING?

Why basic training? Why go through that hell?

Discipline in soldiers, that training does instill.

The marching and drill, what good does it do?

When given orders in combat, you will follow through.

Why the requirement for showing respect for NCO's?

In combat, with your leaders, through hell you may go.

Basic training seems rough, teaches you when to be mean.

Not only must you be alert, but you must fight, as a team.

SUPPORTING UNITS

Deep in the central highlands, my Montagnards and me.

Found our objective, on a ridge in the trees.

Five emplacements for rockets, ready to destroy.

Towards the "A" camp they were aimed, nasty looking toys.

They were set up on a ridge, fifty cal on each flank.

I called in the artillery, we couldn't assault the steep bank.

One o' fives and eight inchers, sent shells overhead.

We swept from their flank, they drag off their dead.

The artillery did their job, trails of blood we could see.

These trails we did track, to engage the enemy.

Darkness fell, we had to stop, security we set out.

A cold camp we did make, the enemy could be about.

At daylight we moved out, the trail we could see again.

Thump-thump we heard the sound, mortar rounds did begin.

The "A" camp I did call, "Mortar rounds on the way."

Artillery timed the rounds, then a location they relayed.

We were at the base of the hill, from where the enemy did shell.

The artillery answered back, not a short round fell.

We lifted fire to assault, support from cobras we had then.

Some we had wounded, for the enemy it was the end.

The body count of the enemy, fifty plus the final toll.

To the support we give credit, for saving our souls.

THOSE WHO STAYED HOME

After all these years, I hear you argue and shout,
about a war you didn't like, but know nothing about.
You have read all the articles, formed your own views,
hell you weren't there, what do you have to lose?
You are why we don't speak, try to make you understand,
you have never left your home, to fight in a foreign land.
All that you know is what the media exposed,
the picture they painted helped their profits grow.
But you have never held a soldier after a fight,
knowing damn well he won't make it till night.
Have you ever made promises, you know you can't keep?
You had to say something, or you may start to weep.
There's more to combat than just killing a man,
emotions build up, soon you don't give a damn.
So if you found a way to let others go and fight,
we can't do it but may you sleep well at night.

THRILL OF THE CHASE

I was asked,
I had to stop and think.
Do I miss battle
and living on the brink?
Then I talked with some vets,
it's bored that we are.
There's no excitement,
just stories in a bar.
It wasn't the kill,
but the thrill of the chase.
When would be the day,
we'd stare death in the face?
Both physical and mental,
scars of battle have we.
They may not be pleasant.
but they're ours, don't you see.

TILL THE END

I was leaving Vietnam, the second or third time.
Smiling privates walked past, where I stood in line.
Fresh off the plane, telling what they would do.
I thought to myself, that used to be you.
My first trip was with buddies, I called friends.
I learned after a while, how to close myself in.
As these men walked by, I had the urge to say.
Laugh and joke right now, that feeling won't stay.
In my mind it's not good, to get attached to a friend.
For me it was easier, to stay strangers until the end.

TO MY FAMILY

To my family I apologize, for the grief I have caused.

The inner battle with which I struggle, never took time to pause.

Fear not for my safety, I have finally sought help.

But like rocks on the ground, it's my memories that won't melt.

They are with me for life, I am trying to understand.

How to handle situations, not give anger the upper hand.

Promises, I won't make, but honestly I will try.

With all your love and support, I'm sure I will get by.

Just one final word, listen if you would.

My love was always there, I just covered it good.

TRUST

Listen close, all you people, you will hear our concern.

Something in combat, we veterans did learn.

We knew somehow, that our comrades were there.

We only needed a man's word, for it was battles we shared.

Then we that come home, with dead and wounded on our mind.

Were accused of many things, we withdrew more with time.

How could you understand, why we wouldn't forget.

It was just an excuse, you were willing to bet.

Many families were broken, for the loss of trust.

When we would self-medicate, we were accused of lust.

I can't speak for all vets, but when accused of the game.

I went ahead and played, since I was given the name.

JODY

Jody was a person of fiction, all soldiers knew well.
When we entered the military, of him we heard tell.
While we were away, he was the one.
That would take your girl, and away would run.
Did Jody know, I wonder, or did he even care?
The heartbreak he caused, and the utter despair,

TWIST OF FATE

We were out on patrol,
during the monsoon.
A swollen stream we did cross,
it was just about noon.
The stream I crossed first,
to tie down the rope.
My little people couldn't swim,
hand over hand they did grope.
While the patrol was crossing over,
a man was swept away.
His footing he had lost, in the stream that rainy day.
My gear I did drop, no time to hesitate.
I pulled him from the water, what a twist of fate.
I was trained to hunt and kill, I reacted to the need.
The soldier was alright, from those waters, he was freed.

TWO KINDS OF PAIN

We that have known battle,
sometimes find it hard to grieve.
We know the loss of fellow soldiers,
remember wounds we received.
We don't like to speak,
of those battles of old.
The pain of flesh tearing,
our brothers long since cold.
I too have these memories,
on my mind; it has left a stain.
Which is worse, I think you know,
of these two kinds of pain.

MY REASON

Some can't understand why I went to that war.
Many reasons I have given, many you've heard before.
Was it for the glory, or the medals I might receive?
No. Neither of these reasons, in my country I believe.
America is my homeland, mistakes she may make.
I will stand behind her, when freedom is at stake.
Though you hated Vietnam, in that war we were caught.
I refuse to accept, the loss of Americans was for naught.

WAS IT FAIR?

I cannot speak for others,
For multiple tours I did spend.
It bothered me when others went,
like my brother or a friend.
I could not stand the thought,
of being home, when they were there.
I was trained I spent my time,
somehow it didn't seem fair.
Many did not come home,
where was I when they died there?
I know to you it may sound crazy,
still I wonder, did I do may share?

I SALUTE YOU, NURSES

It's not for the grunts, this story I tell.
But for the nurses, who have done their job well.
When the grunts end up in a hospital, one day.
The nurses make sure, they have a comfortable stay.
To the moans and groans, they listen all night.
They let no one know, of their inner fight.
From a grunt's medals, his story is told.
The duties of a nurse are more valuable than gold.
Heroics, I say, comes not from a gun.
I salute all Vietnam nurses, for a job well done.

WAYS TO FORGET

I've felt that way,
many times before.
Years ago it started,
in a far-off war.
In the field I could fight it,
with my gun.
Back at camp I would drink,
until it was gone.
I have learned since then,
depression they say.
When I felt it at home,
the bottle was the way.
Now to fight that feeling,
it's pills they give.
Need I depend on them.
as long as I live?

WE LIE

The hurt we don't admit,
we say it's a lie.
They're dead and gone,
why should we cry?
Yet the hurt we feel,
We keep buried inside.
Tears we can't show,
we're men with pride.
Memories we still have,
in our dreams at night.
We hear screams from warriors,
who lost the fight.
These memories will attack us,
until the day we die.
We say we're not bothered,
to ourselves we lie.

WE SHOWED OUR RESPECT

When you're home and your safe, respect you do show.
New suits and ties, in fancy cars you will go.
Flowers will be brought, to place on the grave.
A beautiful headstone, from money they saved.
Respect is not, how much money you spend.
But how you feel, when their life does end.
In combat, our respect we always did show.
Sometimes with a drink, or a party we'd throw.
Empty boots with a prayer, some units would use.
Headgear on a barstool, on the bar, a glass of booze.
However you showed it, it was surely known.
If your time came, respect would be shown.

HARD NOT TO HATE

Vietnam was a war, that will not be forgot.
About thirty years ago, there Americans fought.
To believe in that war, was hard for some.
I find it hard to forgive, what others have done.
If you did not serve, or would not go.
I condemn you not, for your beliefs you showed.
If you left your country, or our flag you did burn.
You disgraced the people, who did not return.
Your feelings toward the war, I can relate.
For disgraceful acts, I find it hard not to hate.

WHAT WAS TAUGHT

They taught us to kill, for war we prepared.
Learn to strike first, you can't hesitate there.
We were taught things, both day and night.
It must be automatic, if you're to win your fight.
For years we served, this country of ours.
Many still carry, their combat scars.
Never were we taught, to unlearn these things.
Trouble and misery, it often did brings.
Sometimes at a bar, when trouble would brew.
From the training we had, the first punch we threw.
We'll take our punishment, should we get caught.
We just try to survive, we do what was taught.

GUILTY CROSS

A lady I know, a neighbor is she.

Was married before, infantry was he.

Many years ago, he did not come home.

About the war she collects, an assortment of poems.

My wife and this lady, are very close friends.

She speaks of her loss, will her agony never end?

Though the war was unpopular, of this I am sure.

To the families of fallen brothers, be strong we'll endure.

For you are not alone, in the feelings of your loss.

We that came home, sometimes bear a guilty cross.

WHY?

Why did I return, when others did not?

Why have MIAs, all but been forgot?

Why was that war, like no other?

Why does that war, politicians bother?

Why do our veterans, have so much anger?

Why did our country, treat us like strangers?

Why do we miss, the fighting and the fear?

Why can't we let, loved ones get near?

Why can't we sleep, at night in our beds?

Why is this confusion, still in our heads?

Why can't we forget, that war long ago?

Why do our families, still love us so?

IT'S NOT DONE

I awoke in a sweat, from another bad dream.
I felt so mixed up, I wanted to scream.
About two weeks ago, I was involved in a wreck.
Another car, I did hit, where two roads intersect.
This I was dreaming, I remember it well.
In my dream after the crash, I heard someone yell.
Get out watch the blades, move away from this bird.
With my weapon I scrambled, following orders I had heard.
At that moment I awoke; I, of course had no gun.
My heart pounding last, my war is not done.

THE INFANTRY

Rockets and mortars,
small arms and large shells.
Years ago in our war,
around us they fell.
At close quarters we fought,
we would die, if need be.
Our job was to light,
we were the infantry.
For the support we received,
we gave credit all around.
Final victory was up to us,
the infantry on the ground.
We saw it up close,
the death and the pain.
Infantry we were,
we fought with no shame.

AIRBORNE AND FEAR

Army airborne training was difficult for me,
it wasn't the running or even the PT.
When it came to heights, I was terrified back then,
even after jump school, I would have to jump again.
You must face your fears, I was told, even as a boy,
I thought that in jump school, week three no joy.
This fear I had to face, for my own sake,
I had to pay attention, no time for mistakes.
Then week three came, time for our first jump
I was scared as hell, how my heart did pump.
The green light came on, out the door, into the sky.
I had so much fun, when I finally opened my eyes.
Those days are long gone, the fun I remember then,
I wore my wings proudly, I was an airborne man.

THE RANGERS

The army has a select few men.
Who are good enough for, the rangers, to be in.
Their course of training, over eight weeks long.
It's a physical course, makes you mentally strong.
For over eight weeks, you will get little rest.
They teach soldiers to lead, while under stress.
Fighting men are these, in many wars they have been.
If they are beaten down, they'll be back again.
Becoming a ranger, is a long hard ride
I earned my tab, I wore it with pride.

THE ARTILLERY

When the infantry is hit, with odds against them.
It's the artillery they call, one shell kills many men.
I've used them myself, in battles I have fought.
These men receive no glory, for their accurate onslaught.
When you are making no headway, your
enemy you want weakened.
Call the artillery, they'll leave them grief stricken.
So keep those guns roaring, on through the night.
It's the infantry you're protecting, in this murderous fight.
Although we may kid you, please do not despair.
We appreciate the artillery, when those rounds are in the air.

SPECIAL FORCES

These are fighting men, airborne all,
anywhere in the world they go when called.
To one year of training they must go,
their courage and ability by then will show.
Only 5 percent will pass the test,
then, you will know you're among the best.
They're trained to fight anytime of the day,
these troopers earn the right, to wear the Green Beret.
During Vietnam with these warriors I served time,
many a brave trooper placed his life on the line.
I made it back to the world, I'm home to stay,
proud to have served, with the Green Berets.

PEOPLE LIKE US

Sorry if we scare you, by the way that we act.

The experiences we had, are a matter of fact.

We that came home, learned to survive in a war.

The remarks that we heard, we admit, made us sore.

You said, "People like us, never again, could fit in."

We tried very hard, for a new life to begin.

Many jobs you refused us, because veterans we were.

But you couldn't keep us down, survivors we are.

Crazy things we still do, we might fight and cuss.

It shouldn't surprise you, you expected it of us.

THE COOK

You want to hear grumbling,
see troops in a bad mood.
Tell them you're sorry,
there is no more food.
Troops returning from the field,
thinking of their plight.
Who do they look for?
That man in cook whites.
They've had their field rations,
for too many days.
Now the thought of real food,
is their mainstay.
When you are in line,
at the mess hall next time.
Appreciate that cook,
without him you don't dine.

RESPECT FOR MEDICS

The Special Forces medic, them I respect.
Some of the best trained, as you might expect.
It's not a rumor, there were no heroics from me.
One incident I remember, listen you'll agree.
I was walking point, with my Montagnard men.
When shots rang out, an ambush we were in.
Three soldiers went down, others went on line.
Two wounded moved back, to fight another time.
"Get Charlie, off our butt," then "Medic!" I did yell.
The fallen soldier, I went to, he was shot all to hell.
Then out of nowhere, this medic did appear.
His bag he did drop, went to work in high gear.
Rounds were still flying, he spoke very few words.
"You son of a bitch don't die," was all that I heard.
I didn't think that medic, could keep him alive.
Thanks to his skill that soldier did survive.

COMBAT ENGINEER

Construction worker is the outside name.

Combat Engineer, in the military, are the same.

A unit first hits country, with no place to rest.

These men of construction, will meet the test.

My brother was one, I'm proud to say.

The work that they did, was hard every day.

Out in the jungle, of that war torn land.

Camps were built, all over Vietnam.

The engineers went in, to clear off the sites.

Fields of fire, they would clear, in case of a fight.

If the enemy should strike, before the jobs end.

Warriors they became, these mighty men.

From the times of our fathers, up to today.

Combat Engineers, a big role do they play.

If it's needed in combat, if construction it takes.

Engineers will be there, make no mistake.

CHOPPER CREWMEN

The infantry looks up and thinks, those guys are nuts.
To be a member of a crew on a chopper, takes guts.
They'll save you from walking, to get to a fight.
To supply you in battle, they fly with all their might.
Many a grunt, they have pulled from deaths jaws.
Flying in support, of the ground pounders cause.
When a chopper goes down, from enemy fire.
The safety of the crew, is a grunt's only desire.
Crewmen, your prowess is known throughout the land.
Hold your head high, you're one hell of a man.

THE MEDIC

Medic or corpsman,
whichever they are.
Are the most popular men,
on the battlefield by far.
A twist of fate,
has given them their skill.
Their job is to save lives,
while we're trained to kill.
If you're in agony and pain,
they'll hear your groan.
Then risk their lives,
to make sure you go home.

REMFs

Ask any Vietnam veteran, if REMFs they have seen.

Rear Echelon Mother F——ers, is what it does mean.

Those were the people, who stayed in the rear.

To run headquarters and offices, I hear.

Most did their job, they did their job well.

Some made up stories, of battles they would tell.

Those were the ones, that irritated us most.

Never saw combat, but how they would boast.

They bragged about missions, they had never been on.

All the way From Saigon, up to Khe Son.

They would tell of rounds flying, capturing enemy loot.

When you looked down, you'd see a spit shined boot.

REMFs, don't speak of false battles and your strife.

You're demeaning our brothers, who gave up their life.

NURSES GIVE HOPE

I awoke in a hospital,
the first face, I did see.
Was a military nurse,
looking down at me.
Half of my body,
in Vietnam had been burned.
She went about her business,
I saw her concern.
The pain and the agony,
I remember to this day.
Words of encouragement,
those nurses did say.
We're sending you home.
to a son you've never seen.
They'd look at his pictures,
I was only nineteen.
If I live to be one hundred,
those nurses, I'll adore.
They gave me hope,
while death knocked at my door.

TWENTY-FIFTH ANNIVERSARY

Radio, television, and even the press, will
cover the anniversary this year.
Twenty-five years since the fall of Saigon, over there,
the communists will cheer.
Americans left there, in seventy-five, for
both sides it was a hell of a cost.
Fifty-eight thousand Americans died there,
It's said three million enemy were lost.
I do not hate the enemy I fought, like me they did as they were told.
I have no desire to return to that land, it
would only open wounds of old.
Politicians and big business ran that war,
the military had very little to say.
If politicians would have stayed at their desk,
that war would not have ended that way.
The biggest disappointment, I think for me,
again this is my point of view.
Was the way our country treated our vets,
it was as if were foreign to you.
The media will take advantage of this event,
the war to which many of us did go.
Because of that war, politicians I don't trust and
resentment for Jane Fonda, I still show.

WOON

I remember a time many years ago.
The battles were fierce and movement was slow.
In the jungles we fought, with our Montagnard men.
For weeks on end, they were our only friend.
In February of seventy, just south of Plei Mrong.
My radioman Woon was played his last song.
A round through his head, in an ambush that day.
Sent Woon to a place, where brave soldiers must stay.
No more may I turn and ask Woon for the mike.
To call for support, for the ongoing fight.
On the ground at my feet, his limp body lies.
The vision still haunts me, to this very day.
What could I have done, to prolong his young life?
This turmoil inside me, has caused me much strife.
When I think back, on the loss of a friend.
I protect myself, it won't happen again.
A loner I've seen, since those days of old.
Some say I am callous, uncaring, and cold.
My days are numbered, I know it will end.
Then I'll see Woon, the soldier I called friend.

SIGHT

Close your eyes, fellow veterans,
it's there, can you see.
That war we were in,
they made for you and me.
See the jungle so thick,
that it blocks out the sun.
See the enemy movement,
now look down at your gun.
It's made of plastic and metal,
but much closer than a friend.
Of it, you took care,
on it your life did depend.
Now look around see the faces,
blank stares, is there fright?
Open your eyes see the tears,
for those left in that fight.

SOUND

Listen to the cheerful sounds, you can hear them every day.

People talking and laughing, little children at play.

In combat you listen, for other kinds of sounds.

You walk quietly and listen, while patrolling on the ground.

Periodically, you must stop, you speak not a word.

You would learn very quickly, if it was the enemy you heard.

You hear the snap of dry wood, maybe the rustle of leaves.

This can cause mothers at home, for their sons to grieve.

Not always did we see the enemy, that we fought.

In ambushes, we set up, many enemy were caught.

They too would use an ambush, I hear the sounds in my head.

Still I hear the choppers, coming for our wounded and dead.

MY REQUEST

I ask of my family, when my time comes to go.
Cremate my remains, before I'm put in a hole.
A military funeral, is what I request.
A bugler in the background, when they lay me to rest.
On my headstone these words, I want laid in stone.
A troubled Veteran he was, now he's resting at home.

TASTE

In combat, there is one thing, you learn not to waste.
The food you are issued, though bad it sometimes tastes.
American units had field rations, they do remember yet.
Americans in Special Forces, ate with our Montagnard men.
We ate indigenous rations, we ate our rice, just like them.
Our little people were crafty, at survival they were smart.
Never did they go hungry, hunting to them was an art.
Snakes and monkey they would kill and boil in a pot.
Small deer and bamboo rat, they did like a lot.
Chicken and fish they would buy, for a small price.
All these things we learned to eat, along with our rice.
Nothing that they hunted went to waste, this we knew.
Chicken guts were cleaned and cut, then boiled in a stew.
All these things I have eaten, though they may not sound so great.
I have now learned to appreciate, a good Porterhouse Steak.

FEEL

Every part of your body, in combat you must use.

Feel the breeze on your face, the ground beneath your shoes.

On your back feel the rucksack, full of things you will need.

Food and water, extra ammo, some explosives for the trees.

Magazines on your web gear, with canteens and snap links.

Hand grenades and a knife, you can grab in a blink.

In your hands, feel your weapon, touch the long narrow bore.

Steel and plastic was all she was, she protected you in that war.

When a firefight would commence, you

would feel the excitement build.

Call for fire on the enemy, for your comrades, on the battlefield.

The wounded, you make your way to, stop the bleeding if you can.

Feel the blood drying sticky, as it flows over your hands.

Feel the weight of the wounded, as they're moved to a safer place.

For those that gave their all, feel the tears run down your face.

SIXTH SENSE

Senses, I have spoken of, in past things I have wrote.

Many times we had to use them, of yet another I have not spoken.

You cannot see, hear, or smell, nor can you taste, or even feel.

Men of combat know, it exists, to them this thing is real.

Call it an instinct, or a sixth sense, or pick another name to give.

If not for this awareness, many warriors would not have lived.

What is this thing? You may wonder, I do not know nor do I care.

I am grateful, whatever it is, for the enemy was killed and I am here.

WE STILL FIGHT

We left Vietnam many years ago,
and still we look back.
The sounds of chopper blades,
reminds us of those bloody attacks.
Experiences there would make blood run cold,
the things we witnessed we still don't share.
We were ridiculed and shamed, here at home.
we refuse to show how much we care.
We're getting old, feelings we still have,
we let it show, when we're not treated right.
When cornered, watch out, we won't back down,
we won't always win, but we'll stay in the fight!

WE SHARE

Feeling sorry for myself,
again the other night.
For no apparent reason,
nothing seemed to go right.
These are the times,
anger swells up inside.
I have tried to control it,
there is no place to hide.
I asked my dear wife,
why she stayed with me?
She held me close and said,
I know what others can't see.
When I was a young man,
to go to war, I did dare.
Now the pain and the agony,
my wife too, does share.

YOUR UNCLE JIM

It's difficult for me to write, I do it for them.
Asked to write by my children, about their Uncle Jim.
We went to high school together, in our younger days.
With cars, girls, and sports, was all we thought to play.
In the army after graduation, I decided to enlist.
First trip to Vietnam I was burned, it was fates twist.
While convalescing at home, because of my burns.
Jim stopped by, his look was stern.
In the army by then, on his way to the war.
Assigned to the first CAV, what was in store?
Make it light, I did try, "An accident I had."
The only way, said he, I'll return will be dead.
"That way, you can't think!" exclaimed I to Jim.
Stay alert, think positive, in that way you'll win.
In Tet of Sixty-Eight, that's the time he passed away.
Tears build up inside me, as I think about that day.
Asked by his mother, if Jim's body I would escort.
To receive his remains, I went to Oakland Port.
At the graveside to his mother, our hag I did present.
I was honored she would ask, a harder day I've never spent.
Two more tours to Vietnam, how my family cringed.
Years later, I now know, in part it was revenge.
You're in the thoughts of your family, like when it all began.
Rest in peace fellow warrior, no more fights for Uncle Jim.

I UNDERSTAND, DAD

My father is a Veteran, of World War Two.
In the Pacific he built airstrips, for those who flew.
My brother and I, in Vietnam, we both served.
Combat accounts, for us all, we keep reserved.
All that we heard, of my father's war.
Was what Grandpa told, for Dad it was a chore.
We understand now, why Dad speaks not.
For years he's tried, that war to be forgot.
I'm not ashamed, to Vietnam I did go.
Now I understand Dad, the healing is slow.

ANGRY I AM

Three times I did go, to that theater of war.
I've been called a murderer, baby killer, and more.
No soldier that went there, started that fight.
We believed in our country, with all our might.
Your trooper I was, you trained me to kill.
I have fought in the jungles, watched men die in those hills.
You think less of me, for what I have done.
But you trained me how, to destroy with a gun.
I apologize not, for the enemy I destroyed.
I was trained to stay alive, that weapon wasn't a toy.
Hell no I'm not happy, it's angry I am.
Can you rid me of my thoughts? You sent me to Vietnam.

A FAMILY LOSS

Every generation
veterans have said, to their kids.
We hope you don't learn of war,
the way that we did.
Anytime there is a battle,
lives will be lost.
It is hard for those at home,
to accept such a cost.
Responsibility has our country,
this we know is true.
Pain this does not ease,
if the loss comes home to you.
If such a loss you have known,
though the memories, still remain.
We that fought beside your loved ones,
also know the pain.

BAGGAGE CHECK

We were laughing and joking, some Vietnam Vets.
Why multiple tours, what did you forget?
Then one man laughed, "It was baggage," said he.
Later I thought, it was true I could see.
Three tours I did serve, though morbid it sounds.
A lot of baggage I left, on those battlegrounds.
Not the kind you can carry onto a plane.
The kind you shove back, deep in your brain.
When it came time to go home, after my tour.
There was no excitement, of this I am sure.
Volunteer I would, for revenge and the thrill.
Would I Check all my baggage, on the next hill?

GO TO HELL

We have nothing at all, to prove to you.
We did very well, what we were trained to do.
If you did not fight, you think that we care'?
It matters not to us, that you were not there.
Yet you are the ones, who still want to know.
What happened in that war thirty years ago?
It is popular now, to be a combat vet.
Our war we refuse, to let you forget.
When we came home, your back you did turn.
If you're upset that we served, go to hell and burn.

IT WASN'T HER FIGHT

I married my wife, some years back.
Sometimes, she feels she is under attack.
My mood swings for me, are hard to contain.
Sometimes she feels, she is to blame.
From my outburst and anger, she does know.
There is something inside me, I cannot control.
Vietnam experiences, still haunt my nights.
She tries to understand but it wasn't her fight.
Through counseling now, I'm doing my best.
I still don't discuss, everything in my past.
So now I write down, these things I can't say.
I let my wile read, what I write every day.
A lot of problems I have, I do not deny.
On her love and support, is what I rely.

HE TRIES

Ask any family member,
of a Vietnam vet.
If he is the same,
a when he first left.
Don't be surprised,
if you hear them say.
He is nothing like
when he left on that day.
He refuses to talk,
keeps everything inside.
How can he understand
why he survived?
There are times he can't control,
his anger or grief.
Try as he might,
nothing grants him relief.

FENCED YARD

Combat veterans don't think like you do.

Most are protective, of what's theirs, it's true.

Not just material things, do I talk bout.

Their mind is a fenced yard, they say who's in or out.

Depending on the person and their mental ghosts.

They will decide, if they will let you get close.

Inside this fenced yard, they are in control.

It's how they survived, not because they are cold.

It there's a veteran you like, to know them is hard.

Try to understand them, it may open their fenced yard.

AWAKE IN THE NIGHT

I awake in the night,
something inside.
Forces me to check,
the doors and window slides.
Before we go to bed,
all the locks we do check.
Why do I awaken?
Am I becoming a mental wreck?
Once I make sure,
every latch is in its place.
I can return to my bed,
For a while mental peace.

DESTRUCTIVE ROAD

A hell-raiser I was, in my childhood years,
all those who knew me would agree.
Many times my family did wondered, what could it be,
that was wrong with me?
Often times, while in my younger years,
I would fail to fall in the mold.
Trouble for me, wasn't hard to find, I just
wouldn't do what I was told.
I toned it down, for a short while, during my high school years.
After graduation, I joined the army, this
caused the shedding of tears.
I drove my family crazy, what would be next, they never knew.
To please them, wasn't my objective, I did only what I wanted to do.
Nine years I served, three tours to war, I never spoke of those times.
No one I felt could ever understand,
the drinking helped to numb my mind.
For years I was on a destructive road, the
wife I now have cares for me.
She's helped me to trust and feel again,
more thoughtful she helps me to be.
The troubles I have, the love she gave, for her it was hard to endure.
Had she not believed and stayed by me,
by now I'd be buried, I'm sure.

INNER PEACE

Inner peace, for a long time, we haven't had.
Thoughts from our past, sometimes make us feel bad.
Young men we were, during the Vietnam days.
The war was real, it was our game to play.
Death and destruction, we inflicted over there.
Then we held it inside, those things we wouldn't share.
When we came home, our families couldn't know.
Why we had changed, affection was hard to show.
Our mood swings are drastic, often lonely we get.
Medication they give, helps the depression in vets.
Do all veterans, we wonder, feel out of place?
Are we just waiting to die to find inner peace?

BATTLES AND GHOSTS

Many combat veterans can still here the cry.
Asleep in their bed, where they lie.
This is the time it troubles them most.
The battles they fought return of their ghosts.
It's hard to go on, but most fight the curse.
Some have ended it all, which is worse?
I do not condemn them, if this way they did choose.
Their loved ones now, are the ones that lose.
I know not their feelings, most could not explain.
The feeling of depression, set so deep in their brain.

LEND A HAND

If our way of life was threatened,
what would you do?
Would you serve our country,
could we depend on you?
If the draft was reinstated,
to protect America's might.
Would you serve or find a way,
to let others go and fight?
I just can't understand,
some people in this land.
To insure our way of life,
we must all lend a hand.
If you can forget those who died,
in some far off foreign place.
How can you, without shame,
look yourself in the face?

TEARS IN MY EYES

You can't cry, you're a man, I've been told.

Sometimes it is hard, these tears to hold.

But I am a man, emotions we don't show.

These are the teachings, I had long ago.

Then around Veterans Day, this past year.

A call from my granddaughter, caused my eyes to tear.

Of war and our veterans, in school she did learn.

Her mother explained, your grandpa had his turn.

Not a question did she ask, my little Morning Star.

Said she, thank you, Papa, for fighting in that war.

We've all waited for acknowledgement, in some small way.

From those few words, my tears did fall that day.

ALONE HE SITS

Alone he sits at the table,
this Vietnam vet wonders if he is able.
Can he make it through another day?
Depression he has, so they say.
If not for his family and his wife,
he fears that he would take his life.
Other veterans he knew long before,
ended their life because of that war.
Judge them he won't, these brave men,
he understands, the turmoil they were in.

THAT LOOK

What's the matter with you? I heard someone say.
Aren't you proud, of all the battles you fought?
I turned to see, if he was speaking to me.
I knew of combat, this gentleman knew not.
"Why would you think," I then asked of him.
"I would be proud, of that death and gore?"
"I am not ashamed, but proud is a strong word,
you'd know, if you had been in combat before."
I'm curious said he, how could have known,
that in combat I never had to serve?
First was the question that you ask of me.
Second, you don't have that look, no man deserves.

ARE WE ALONE?

Still I sit and wonder, I ask myself why
Are warriors born, are they predestined to die?
Or is it simple mistakes, that will take their life?
Leaving small children, a loved one or a wife.
None chose to die, from the ravages of war.
Every soldier gave his all, how could we even the score?
Time marches on, our mind unwilling to let go.
We replay in our sleep, a real combat show.
The fighting goes on, for those who made it home.
We have questions, no answers, are we alone?

TIME TO MEND

Oftentimes I do wonder,
about these faces I see.
At night they appear while I sleep,
what I wonder do they want from me?
I recognize their uniforms,
and the weapons they carry.
Though the names I can't recall,
some of these faces I know are buried.
Out of the night old memories return,
of battles in a war that was our hell.
These things, I never would speak of,
of these experiences, I never would tell.
What is it that you warriors want?
There is nothing I can do old friend.
To the veterans, are they trying to say,
the time has come for your guilt to mend.

TIME AFTER TIME

Where did all,
the warriors go?
Those who fought
so long ago.
Many from that war,
were laid to rest.
Both living and the dead,
they did their best.
We that returned,
to face the scorn.
Wished at times,
for us they mourned.
You know not,
what is in our minds.
We relive that war,
time after time.

IS THAT YOU?

They're still in my brain, those days long past.
Those that fell, I hope, finally found rest.
To grieve is a thing, we that are left must learn.
If we are to go on, for it is not yet our turn.
It was anger I felt, when your lives you did lose.
I have no one to blame, for to fight I did choose.
Dreams I do have, of the fighting and the screams.
Deceased though you are, is that you in my dreams?

THOUGHTS

I was out by a lake,
on the shore I did stand.
A chopper flew overhead,
the hair on my neck did stand.
The sound of those blades,
moving swiftly through the air.
Brought back the memories,
and feelings of utter despair.
It is strange how a thought,
maybe a sound, or even a smell.
Can propel your mind back, to a place,
that for you was pure hell.

THE WALL

I have been asked,
if I've been to the wall.
The Vietnam Memorial,
for those who did fall.
No, I haven't been,
nor did I want to go.
The anger I fear,
inside me would grow.
Veterans I know,
believe that I should.
The memories I have,
were not always good.
If to the wall I don't go,
somehow in my brain.
Fallen men will come back,
like the monsoon rain.

WE DON'T TALK

At the end of sixty-seven, my brother Dan, did leave.

I was recovering from burns, in Nam I received.

To the hundred and first, Dan was assigned.

I was proud, but worried, for brother of mine.

Like others, when he returned different was he.

A little wilder, a lot older, a loner you could see.

We never talked, of our experiences there.

Only the drinking, bar fights and parties, did we share.

After all these years, about Vietnam, we don't talk.

Each of us knows, the others hell we have walked.

WHAT DOES IT SAY?

What does it say, that memorial they made?
The Vietnam memorial, for all the lives paid.
Does it say for democracy, all those names fought?
To me this question, it answers not.
For liberty tell me, did those names give their life?
How many of those names, had children or a wife?
Does our country feel, those names died in vain?
The wall tells us not, of their suffering and pain.
For many the wall helps, I have heard said.
The wall says to me, those warriors are dead.

WAR STORY

While sitting in a bar, one lonely night.

A man asked to hear, of a combat fight.

War stories I don't tell, I said to him.

He kept on persisting, so I said with a grin.

We were deep in the jungle, during the monsoon.

Five Montagnards and I, must have been around noon.

Surrounded by the enemy, they were coming up the hill.

Weather delayed the choppers, support was nil.

We ran out of ammo, then rocks we did throw.

"What happened?" the man asked, his face all aglow.

It's hard to speak of, I hate this next part.

Overran us they did, then they cut out our hearts.

IF IT WERE YOU

If you were too young, to have fought over there.

I do not write to make you despair.

We have fought in a war, unpopular to most.

Many a fine warrior gave up his ghost.

In battles we fought, blood and pain we did see.

Now stop and think, what if that were me?

How would you react, if during the night?

Years later, in your dreams, you relived those fights.

It's not war that we glorify, nor do we brag.

Was it really old-fashioned, to serve our flag?

YOU TOOK OUR PRIDE

Ask any Vietnam veteran,
he will answer back loud.
For his country he served,
of this he was proud.
When he returned from that war,
he was ridiculed and shamed.
For the death and destruction,
each of us were blamed.
We have lived many years.
not knowing what to do.
Depression fills our souls,
many have turned to booze.
Alcohol drowns our thoughts,
we know not where to hide.
Proud warriors we were once,
you took our pride.

YOU HAVEN'T THE RIGHT

Young people in our military,
no matter what branch.
Come from all walks of life:
small towns, cities, or maybe a ranch.
Why must some, put them down?
It's our country, they serve.
Many have died, on foreign ground,
It's our support our military deserve.
In numerous wars we have engaged,
many gave their life in the fight.
Protest if you must, do not degrade,
"You, sir, haven't earned that right!"

YOUR MIND WON'T YIELD

Have you ever saw someone, out on the street?
The face you recognize, but the memory is not complete.
Then later you feel, you have entered a dark cloud.
It embraces your soul, wraps you, like deaths shroud.
Then it floods your mind, where you saw that face before.
The face you thought you recognized was from that bloody war.
But that could not be, he was dead in that field.
The guilt creeps over you, your mind, will never yield.
Is it punishment you wonder, for remorse, that you lack?
In your mind you hold the guilt, because you made it back.

YEARS HAVE PASSED

Many a night I lay on the land,
looking at the stars over Vietnam.
I've been home now for many a year,
still unable to shed any tears.
The death and destruction I witnessed there,
makes me wonder, how could I not care.
The feelings I have, I cannot explain,
a mixture of anger, sorrow, confusion and pain.
I have no idea, when I can put it to rest,
I honestly try, I'm doing my best.
Sometimes my thoughts cause me to rave,
I feel these memories will haunt me to my grave.

WE DID OUR JOB

I don't understand, politicians what's the fuss?

You trained us to be warriors, is it mistrust?

We did our job, the way we were trained.

Fighting and killing, in the heat and the rain.

For years we've been home and problems, have we?

There are barriers to scale, for a doctor to see.

If we're not on the streets, of this there's no doubt.

Politicians want to know, what we're griping about.

For many veterans, daily life is a chore.

We did our job, we ask you do yours.

WELL TRAINED

I have seen men in combat,
kill for the first time.
I did not think, years later,
it would work on their mind.
I went through this myself,
but after a while.
The enemy I could kill,
later manage to smile.
A teenager I was,
when they expanded the war.
Never could I have imagined,
such bloodshed and gore.
Like other Vietnam veterans,
you trained me well.
If the need should arise.
still I could kill.

ARE WE HOME?

We that served in that war and made it back home.

Have been in a crowd and felt all alone.

The memories of Vietnam, made us that way.

If we let no one close, the hurt won't stay.

Though our bodies are here, it's hard to explain.

Our minds still slosh, through monsoon rains.

It can hit anytime, but it's worse at night.

In our dreams we return, to another firefight.

The body is in one place, our minds do roam.

I wonder at times, will we ever be home?

CAN YOU UNDERSTAND?

Few people I know, do I call friend.

Acquaintances I have, both women and men.

It is not the standards, that I set high.

But a defensive measure, learned in years gone by.

At one time there were many, that I called friend.

To me there was no danger, of ever losing them.

When I was young and bold, I was sent off to war.

I had no way of knowing, what lay I store.

I still feel the pain, for those that were lost.

For letting them get close, this pain is the cost.

My emotions for years, I held in somehow.

There are many like me, can you understand now?

DON'T ASK

Can't you tell us of Vietnam?
A young man asked.
What is your problem?
Is to talk such a task?
How can I explain,
a war you know not?
The things that you know,
in school you were taught.
The books will not tell you,
the soldier's point of view.
To tell of our story,
would make you wonder, can this be true?
Ask not us to tell you,
Of death and gore we have seen.
We choose not to talk,
we relive it in our dreams.

ONLY YOU KNOW

A man that I know, a Vietnam vet.
Artillery he was says he can't forget.
Some of my poems, this man had read.
Write what I feel. "I can't," I said.
Stuck on a firebase, is what it was called.
I have no knowledge, of this at all.
For the enemy I looked, I was on the ground.
Not long in one place, we moved all around.
You were stuck in one place, a target you were.
When we called fire missions, rounds would appear.
I would not be correct, if I wrote how you feel.
Only you can say, what to you is real.

TREAT US RIGHT

What do you expect, Vietnam veterans to do?
We're a thorn in your side, that irritates you.
First was agent orange that you did deny.
Now veteran's hospitals, you won't supply.
You think if you tell us there's no money to pay.
We will hang our heads and just go away.
We are not few, there are many of us.
We did our jobs, in our country we did trust.
Those of us who survived, through that bloody fight.
Only ask that America, will now treat us right.

STORMY MEMORIES

Hear the roar of the thunder,
see the lightning flash.
Back come the memories,
of when warriors did clash.
The roar of the thunder,
are like artillery shells.
The hash of the lightning,
are where the shells tell.
The rain too brings back memories,
as it falls on our head.
It's the tears we can't hide,
For our comrades who are dead.

POLITICIANS PROMISES

In election year, there is no mistake.

To get our votes, promises you will make.

We ask only one thing, before you proceed.

Veterans benefits leave alone, for those who do need.

You cut and you gouge, you treat you job as a craft.

If we veterans don't stop you, we'll have nothing left.

Beware of broken promises and deals that you make.

A new job you may look for, if our benefits you take.

THAT DREAM

I had a dream last night,
Then I awoke with a start.
A soldier entered my dream,
Said he, "We all did our part."
He had invaded my dream,
"For what?" I asked him to tell.
I am here for your comrades,
Who gave their life, in that hell.
You that made it back home,
Cling to a wall, you have built.
Many years have not passed,
You must get rid of the guilt.
I choked back the tears,
As I tried to explain.
We have tried to be rid,
Of these thoughts, in our brain.
It is a long slow process,
But we are trying old friend.
Until this thing happens,
He'll be back, again and again.

TEARS AND MEMORIES

It is hard for many veterans,
to speak of their war.
Things they have experienced,
is like a festering sore.
They honestly can't remember,
things they chose to forget.
In their sleep it comes together,
tears and memories have met.
Emotions build up inside them,
like a Dam they build a wall.
This Dam holds emotions,
holds the tears so they won't fall.
In later years it starts to haunt them,
For no reason they will cry.
These proud warriors will simply say,
they know not the reason why.

STILL ALIVE

How the time
has slipped away.
The guilt we carry,
is how we pay.
We know that
deep inside our brain.
That Vietnam war,
will always remain.
The horror we saw,
in those days of old.
Would make our families,
blood run cold.
Many brave soldiers
did not survive.
We feel the guilt,
we're still alive.

QUESTIONS?

You weren't there, why are you concerned'?
Why did I go, how did I get burned?
During a fire light, did you show fear?
What a stupid question, let me drink my beer.
But I say not a word, just look through him and smile.
He just keeps on talking, for a very long while.
Then for some reason, he feels the need to explain.
Why he had to work, but he wanted to be a marine.
Out of frustration. he moves down the bar.
A nudge from the man next to me, gives me a jar.
He whispers, they know not our feelings, they think we're still sore.
They just don't realize, we don't care anymore.

THE PAIN

I see them at night,
they come in my dreams.
Young faces of soldiers,
I can still hear their screams.
No names can I remember,
but the pain is still felt.
I awaken not knowing,
why I feel so much guilt.

ON THE EDGE

It's hard for some veterans,
not to live on the edge.
The memories of battles,
are still in their heads.
Although we are home,
and grow older each day.
Like children at times,
dangerous games we must play.
We believe, it's how to have fun,
a rush we will get.
Although dangerous it may be,
we know not how to quit.

HAVE YOU FORGOTTEN?

Have you forgotten nine-eleven, have you so soon forgot the pain?
Many innocent people died that day, as
terrorists brought down a fiery rain.
I defend your right to protest, against a war with Saddam Hussein.
I do not understand, nor do I agree, he
supports those that were to blame.
He has weapons of mass destruction, of which he refuses to be rid.
U.N. Inspectors will never find them, he's
had twelve years to get them hid.
When our military go in to disarm him, let us pray the war is brief.
I know the hell they will go through, let us
support our Commander in Chief.

LONELY NIGHTS

Sometimes I feel lonely, when I turn out the lights.
During the day I am busy, I don't sleep well at nights.
Crazy things I have done, since leaving the war zone.
High and low were my mood swings, after I got home.
Nothing could I find, to put excitement in my life.
Drinking and lighting, would bring agony to my wife.
These things didn't bother me, I called it having fun.
Although, at times from the law I did run.
The older I get, the more depression sets in.
To straighten out my life, where do I begin?
Right now I am not drinking, I avoid the lights.
Still it's not easy, to make it through the nights.

BAD DREAM

He lay there on the battlefield,
many things going through his brain.
He knew he was hit, that's why he fell,
he was surprised, he felt no pain.
A medic dropped down beside him.
he said, "I'll return for you old friend."
Men in pain, he heard their screams,
so off to them he ran.
The sounds of battle did subside.
Not a word did the soldier hear spoke.
Just as he was being placed, in a body bag,
Safe at home in his bed, that veteran awoke.

MANY BROTHERS

If you served in the military, combat or not.
We have a bond, this we were taught.
We combat veterans, are brothers of the soul.
We don't want trouble, peace of mind is our goal.
So if you served in combat, rather I know you or not.
Spread the word many brothers, Combat Veterans have got.

FOR THEM

Listen to these words, I'm about to say.
Give them a thought, when you have a bad day.
When things don't seem to go as they should.
You'd like to give up, you would if you could.
Let me tell you of men, that I once knew.
Who would gladly exchange places with you.
Warriors they were. some still in their teens.
I still see them sometimes, asleep in my dreams.
They gave their all, these men lost their life.
Never enjoying the comfort, of a family or a wife.
So when depression sets in, you start feeling bad.
Keep going for them and the life they never had.

HOPE

War in general, is a bloodthirsty game.
True warriors don't go, for glory or fame.
Our country decides, when it's time to fight.
Kiss loved ones goodbye, then off into the night.
No one knows, how long they'll be gone.
What they'll be like, if they come home?
Many have fought, endured hardships of war.
Hoping that someday, there would be no more.
Bring the symbol of peace, the beautiful white dove.
Let warriors know serenity and feel a family's love.

BUMPER STICKER

From a bumper sticker, I got a chuckle today.
Veterans Do It For Their Country, is what it did say.
In my mind, for some reason, I couldn't forget.
Of another time, when my family did fret.
I can't speak for all, but in my case.
The military I left, Fort Lewis was the place.
Hard to find, was a job, I searched all around.
Steady work driving truck, was all that I found.
Fifty percent disabled, when I did leave.
Burns, wounds and hearing loss, is what I received.
Surely a job I could get, if I would apply.
Then I did learn, veterans preference was a lie.
"Veterans Do It For Their Country," from this I construed.
Our government didn't care if veterans got screwed.

AM I A THREAT?

While driving down the road,
a car cuts in fast.
My heart starts pounding,
the rage just won't pass.
Sometimes it's so bad,
I must pull off the road.
Relax, wipe the sweat,
it helps to unburden my load.
The load of which I speak,
builds in my mind.
I tell myself, to relax,
everything now is fine.
At the moment that it happens,
although I might regret.
The anger is so strong,
to them, am I a threat?

A WAY OUT

Do you not listen
to what we have said.
We do not sleep,
at night in our beds.
We awaken often
from dreams of our past.
You told us not to worry,
it would not last.
A long time ago,
we were told these things.
Now, thirty years later,
depression it brings.
Many of our veterans,
are dead or dying inside.
They felt the only way out,
was a bottle or suicide.

MUST BE A MISTAKE

I still don't understand what's wrong with me.
The life I have led, you say caused PTSD.
Everyone, I thought, who has been in a war.
Are bound to come back, a little bit sore.
There are things I have done, some say were strange.
Do you feel my actions were sometimes deranged?
Fighting and drinking in general raising hell.
Helped me to forget, those I served with who fell.
I have supported my family, I worked all the time.
Extra shifts I would pull, is that out of line.
Few people disliked me, I had no real friends.
Crowds I don't like, facing a door I will stand.
I awake in the night, only three or four times.
Doesn't everyone get up to check the locks and blinds?
Sometimes it is hard to control my anger and depression.
Now you have me attending weekly counseling sessions.
Is there something wrong, the way I lived my life?
You must be mistaken, I still have my second wife.

STARS

I walked out last night,
looked up at the sky.
The stars shined bright,
I thought of years gone by.
I remember from the jungles,
at these same stars I looked.
I thought how beautiful they are,
like a picture from a book.
I used to wonder back then,
do these stars shine at home?
When loved ones looked at them,
did they feel alone?

SILENT RESPECT

We meet Wednesday nights, at the center.
At six this group of veterans, does enter.
From all types of backgrounds we do come,
slowly but surely, we get to know each one.
In many ways different, in some ways the same,
we have all known combat, that was our game.
Just like me, they're not always direct,
each one of these veterans, has my silent respect.

THE WILLING

What is it in the minds
of young men that makes them go?
Is it something they are missing,
or something they must show?
Many cannot be content,
to stay at home, if there's a war.
Even though not a clue,
do they have for what's in store.
I do not put them down,
for I too was such a lad.
To the army I had to go,
against the wishes of my dad.
What I proved was to myself,
it's embedded in my brain.
Our country should be grateful,
for combat, others are willing to train.

THOSE AT HOME

I feel blessed and lucky, I'm here to say.

My children, at war never had to play.

Until now I never gave it much thought.

For those at home, the agony war brought.

Sending one of your children, off to a war.

While you wait at home, must be a chore.

I know as a warrior, what it's like to be.

For my children to witness, I didn't want to see.

People that I know, their child did enlist.

They pray that their child, won't make the next list.

That list of the next group, going off to war.

The thought is always there, they may see them no more.

YOU WERE WRONG

Will the day ever come
we can raise our head high?
Politicians will finally admit,
to the veterans they did lie.
Vietnam was not for freedom,
for big business, lives were paid.
Just admit that you were wrong,
then fallen brothers, at rest may lay.

TROUBLE

Things I have done, since my first trip to Nam.
Six wrecks I've been in and walked away from.
In many altercations. I have been involved.
Drinking and lighting, nothing ever was solved.
Four times I've been in jail, from one to four days.
I refused to admit, I should change my ways.
In counseling now, after a wreck and DUI.
After all these years, PTSD is partly why.
What is this thing that helped wreck my life?
Screwed up my head, almost lost my wife.
Some kind of depression, from combat stress.
The older you get, the more your mind is a mess.

VETERANS CAN RELATE

Angry I sound,
sometimes when I write.
I feel tired and alone,
the war haunts me at night.
I care not if you dislike,
the words that you see.
If one veteran can relate,
that's good enough for me.

HELP ME UNDERSTAND

I ask you please, help me to understand.
Although I have served and fought for our land.
To get business loans, I have tried.
Both times, you have denied.
Yet immigrants will come in.
And you will grant loans to them.
Jobs, they haven't got.
Of course collateral, they have not.
Out of proportion, this has grown.
Why can't we first, take care of our own?

TOO MUCH TO ASK?

Is it ended now, that Vietnam war?

If so, why do the memories last?

Vets with troubled minds, depression set in.

From a war, now thirty years past.

Some of us wonder, why it took so long?

For our country to recognize our need.

Our physical wounds have long since healed.

It's our minds that continue to bleed.

All gave some, some gave all.

Check the wall, you'll see it's true.

The families want help, for their vets.

Do you feel, it's too much to ask of you?

BUSINESS LOAN

Northern California to Sacramento, I did go.

Ten years ago, maybe more I don't know.

A business loan, I hoped I would get.

I served my time, I'm a disabled vet.

The man looked at the papers I had.

Then said he, that is really too bad.

It wasn't the papers, or what I had wrote.

Too new of a business, he thought I'd go broke.

I started to boil, what really set me off.

This little weasel said, with a scoff.

"Because you were there, you Vietnam vets.

You think a free ride, you should get.

I could hold it no longer, I jumped from my chair.

I went for his throat, both my hand were bare.

I tried to grab him, I was stopped by my wife.

I don't think he realized, I wanted his life.

BRIEF OUTLINE

Of things I have written, some experiences I have told.

Of members of my family and battles in a war of old.

Never have I sit and of my life tried to write.

Written only of loved ones and what haunts me at night.

I was born in Yakima, Washington, the year was Forty-Seven.

In Crewport, a farm labor camp, I lived until age seven.

My parents had divorced when I was only six.

A marriage gone bad, things happened they couldn't fix.

My father had custody of one girl and three boys.

A construction worker he was, carpentry he enjoyed.

Then when I was eight, another wife my father found.

Fourteen was my age, when I could no longer stay around.

My sister and her husband, to their home, took me in.

Through high school I did stay, then on my own, I struck again.

Soon after I was married, three months past eighteen.

In the army by then, with a wife I seldom seen.

Two children we did have, they have brought a lot of joy.

Though I wasn't around much, there was a war for us boys.

After nine years, an honorable discharge, I received.

Next, a long haul truck driver, for the money I did need.

Too young, I know now, we were when we wed.

We parted in eighty-five, for different lives we both had.

In eighty six I remarried and she is a wonderful gal.

Through all of my turmoil's, she has been there all the while.

In eighty-eight, when I applied, a government job I did get.

We moved to Southern California, far from where we first met.

A son she lost in eighty-four now our children number four.

Eight grandchildren, we do enjoy, we hope there will be more.

A brief outline of my life, on this paper I have wrote.

Through the hard times, I must admit, my family kept me afloat.

You may wonder of my life, what is it I'm looking for?

Just happiness for my family, them I do adore.

THANKS

Drinking, fighting and wrecks I've been in.

Another Vietnam veteran, called as a friend.

"Get down to the vet center, on sixth," said he.

"Ask for a counselor, it's help that you need."

Who is this man, thinks he knows me so well?

Later I found, he'd been through the same hell.

I went to the center, thought I'd bluff my way through.

The counselor, said she, "your progress is up to you."

I visit her weekly, to her group sessions I've been.

How much progress have I made, to say I can't begin.

The problem I have is called PTSD.

I awake in the night, from dreams I did see.

We talk them all over, my counselor and I.

Slowly but surely. more blue seems the sky.

I know you can't cure me, but for the profession you chose.

For helping this veteran, "Thank You," Paula Rose.

AMERICA'S MIGHT

I don't know of your thoughts, don't care of your views.
Live the way you want, that's for you to choose.
We have people in this land, no matter what we do.
They tell you of our laws, claim they don't protect you.
I like many other men, fought and gave my all.
Though our country is not perfect, she will not fall.
If you ever get a chance, go to a land where you can't speak.
See the ghosts in the eyes, of the people in the streets.
By many countries we are hated, for the freedom our people get.
We are a world power, we've been chosen to baby sit.
If you are an extremist, no matter left or right.
If you think you'll overthrow her, plan to face America's might.

WE ARE AMERICANS

When terrorists struck our country we mourned,
For we are Americans.
When Iraq refused to disarm, we warned,
For we are Americans
Life, Liberty, and Pursuit of Happiness, is our right
For we are Americans.
If these things you try to take, we'll fight,
For we are Americans.
No matter the Color, Creed, or Religion, we defend,
For we are Americans.
We welcome Allies, but on ourselves depend,
For we are Americans.
Let Countries that disagree, take heed,
For we are Americans.
Our Military are a special Breed,
For we are Americans.

AGAIN SENT TO WAR

Young men and women, again sent to war.
Your safe return, is what we pray for.
Though we know, that some will not return.
From your determination, the enemy will learn.
You are ready and willing, to meet the test.
Like many before you, you will do your best.
By terrorists, unprepared we were caught.
That September day will not be forgot.
It's pride you instill, for us here at home.
In the long fight ahead, you are not alone.
Let the enemy know, with each rising sun.
The colors in our flag, will never run.

ABOUT THE AUTHOR

Ronnie V. Nash graduated from high school in 1965 in Granger, Washington. In 1965, at the age of seventeen, he enlisted in the US army. In 1966, he completed airborne training in Wiesbaden, Germany, and volunteered to go to Vietnam. After training with Delta Company, 51ST Prov. Infantry, Fort Lewis, Washington, they shipped out for Vietnam in October of 1966. In March of 1967, he was severely burned over; 55 percent of his body during an accidental gasoline explosion. In 1968, he applied for and was accepted for Special Forces training at Fort Bragg, North Carolina. He graduated from SF training in 1969 and volunteered for a second tour in Vietnam.

Nash served with II Corps MIKE force out of Pleiku and as the Intel Sgt. at Ben Het, it Special Forces "A" camp, in the tri-border area of II Corps. He returned to Fort Bragg in late 1970. In early 1971, he applied for and was accepted into the Ranger training school at Fort Benning, Georgia. He received his Ranger tab in April of that same year. He volunteered for Vietnam again (third tour) in 1972.

On his third tour, he was involved in the training of Cambodians, Vietnamese Rangers, and Recon teams. In February 1973, they were called out of the field. He volunteered for the Joint Casualty Resolution Center in Thailand. We worked in five-man teams, going into Vietnam, unarmed, searching for MIA's most of whom were downed pilots. During his tours of duty in Vietnam, he was the recipient of the following decorations for my combat actions: Silver Star, Bronze Star, Air Medal for valor, Purple Heart, and the Vietnamese Cross of Gallantry. He was honorably discharged in March 1974.

He was a cross-country truck driver until 1988. He went to work for the U.S. Customs service in 1988. He retired from the U.S. Customs Service in March of 2000, and he now resides in Hanford, California, with his family.

Ronnie V. Nash

CPSIA information can be obtained
at www.ICGtesting.com
Printed in the USA
FSOW02n2020091116
27210FS